PROUD TO BE AN
AMERICAN

Lee Greenwood

Illustrated by Amanda Sekulow

Clovercroft Publishing

Proud to Be an American

© 2015 by Lee Greenwood

Published by Clovercroft Publishing, Franklin, Tennessee

Illustrations by Amanda Sekulow and Daniel Pagan (Assistant Illustrator)

Cover and Interior Design by Suzanne Lawing

Edited by Paul Shepherd

Additional Editing by Alice Sullivan

Printed in the United States of America

978-1-940262-96-3

Growing up on my grandparents' farm in California gave me an appreciation for folks who worked hard and got by on very little. The saving grace was that I didn't know we had very little. My grandparents lost their farm after government regulations prevented them from farming the more profitable fields. But they didn't question why it happened; they just started a new business. They trusted that America would hold true to the promise that freedom gives you choices. They believed that no matter what difficulties we experienced as a family, we would be okay because we were free.

Music always inspired me and kept me focused on the future. When the United States was in the depths of conflict, I felt an obligation to make a difference with my music and bring pride back to our country. Nearly twenty years later, I moved to Nashville, Tennessee, to become a recording artist and after three years of touring, I wrote "God Bless the USA."

America is still the greatest country on earth. This book is meant to reinforce the same patriotism and optimism in our children and grandchildren I felt as a young boy. As you sit together reading the words of my song to your child or grandchild, and viewing the illustrations that reflect the lyrics, it is my hope that young and old alike will feel tremendous pride in being citizens of the United States of America.

LEE GREENWOOD

If tomorrow all the things were gone
I'd worked for all my life.

And I had to start again
with just my children and my wife.

I'd thank my lucky stars
to be livin' here today.

'Cause the flag still stands for freedom
and they can't take that away.

From the lakes of Minnesota,

to the hills of Tennessee

Across the plains of Texas,

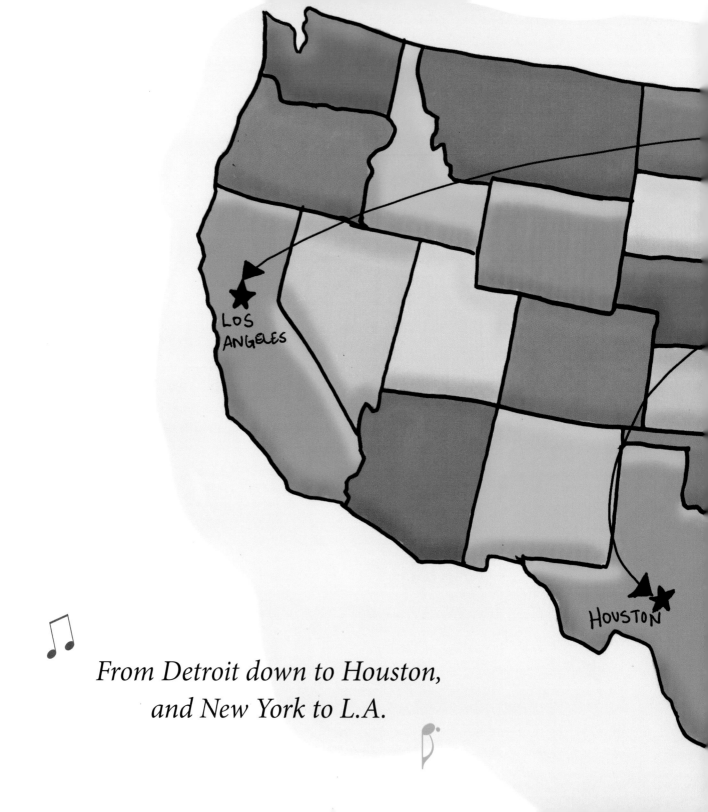

From Detroit down to Houston,
and New York to L.A.

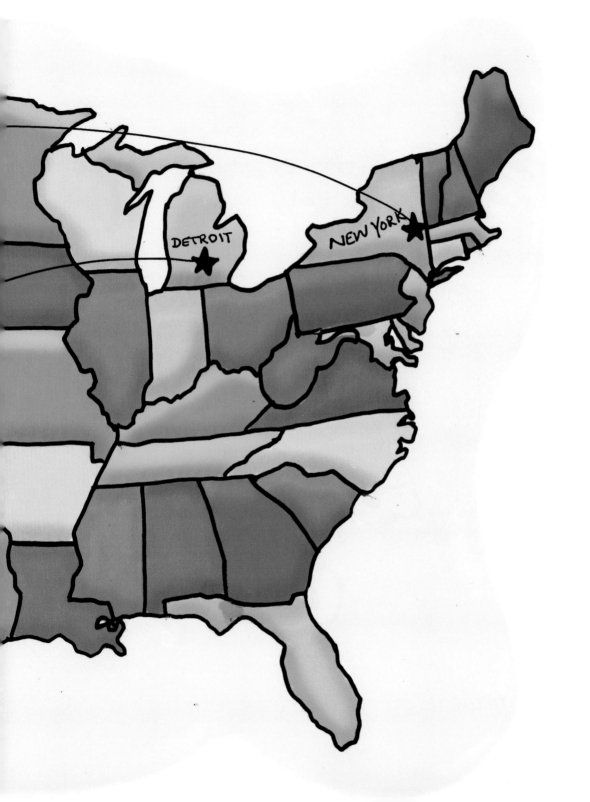

♩

There's pride in every American heart

♪

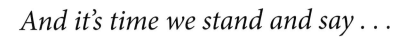

And it's time we stand and say . . .

I'm proud to be an American
where at least I know I'm free.

And I won't forget the men who died,

♫ *who gave that right to me.* ♪

And I'd gladly stand up next to you
and defend Her still today.

'Cause there ain't no doubt I love this land.

God bless the USA.

GOD BLESS THE U.S.A.

Text adapted for
Proud to Be an American

If tomorrow all the things were gone
I'd worked for all my life
And I had to start again
With just my children and my wife

I'd thank my lucky stars
To be living here today
'Cause the flag still stands for freedom
And they can't take that away

And I'm proud to be an American
Where at least I know I'm free
And I won't forget the men who died
Who gave that right to me
And I'd gladly stand up next to you
And defend Her still today
'Cause there ain't no doubt
I love this land
God bless the U.S.A.

From the lakes of Minnesota
To the hills of Tennessee
Across the plains of Texas
From sea to shining sea

From Detroit down to Houston
And New York to L.A.
There's pride in every American heart
And it's time we stand and say

That I'm proud to be an American
Where at least I know I'm free
And I won't forget the men who died
Who gave that right to me
And I'd gladly stand up next to you
And defend Her still today
'Cause there ain't no doubt
I love this land
God bless the U.S.A.

And I'm proud to be an American
Where at least I know I'm free
And I won't forget the men who died
Who gave that right to me
And I'd gladly stand up next to you
And defend Her still today
'Cause there ain't no doubt
I love this land
God bless the U.S.A.

I dedicate this book to:

Jesus Christ for His never-ending grace.

*Kim, my beautiful wife, who continues to
teach me the true meaning of love.*

*Dalton & Parker, my sons, who show honor to this family
and to their country in everything they say and do.*

*My grandparents who taught me wrong from right
and gave me the chance to find my destiny.*

*Our military that sacrifices beyond measure
for the freedoms we enjoy every day.*

God Bless the USA!

Lee Greenwood